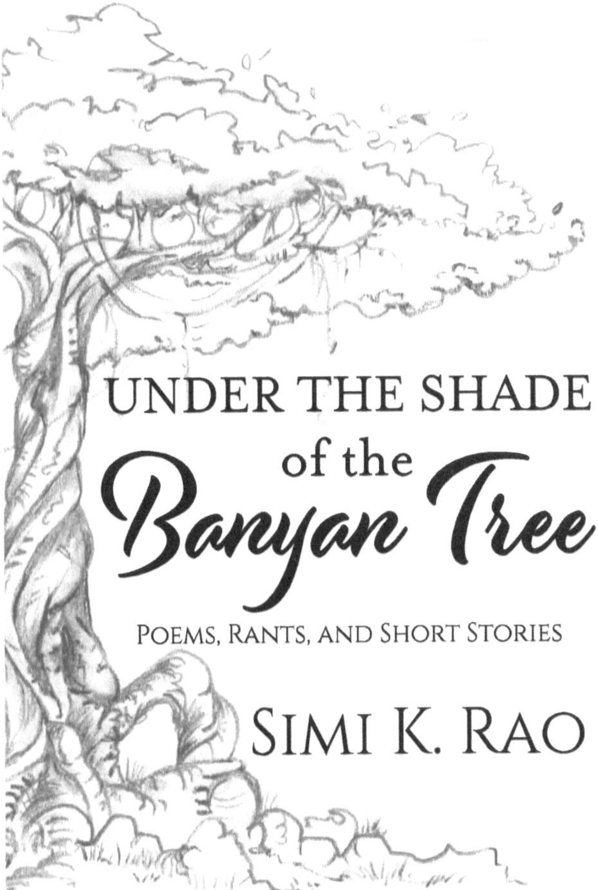

UNDER THE SHADE of the Banyan Tree

POEMS, RANTS, AND SHORT STORIES

SIMI K. RAO

Written Dreams Publishing

Green Bay, WI 54311

Under the Shade of the Banyan Tree: Poems, Rants, and Short Stories by Simi K. Rao, copyright © 2019 by Simi K. Rao. Author Photo courtesy of the Rao family, © 2019 by the Rao Family. "A River" and "Crush," an excerpted from *Inconvenient Relations* by Simi K. Rao, copyright © 2016 by Simi K. Rao. Reprinted by permission of the author. Illustrations, including the illustration on the cover art design © 2019 by Amanda Dix. The cover art design, interior layout design, and chapter head artwork, and logo of Written Dreams Publishing © 2019 by Written Dreams Publishing.

This is a collection of poems and short stories based on the reflections about life by Simi K. Rao. All poems and short stories are works of fiction. All names, characters, places, and events are products of the author's imagination or are used fictitiously, and any resemblance to actual persons, living or dead, or to actual places or businesses, is entirely coincidental. Written Dreams Publishing does not approve, condone, or disapprove of the situations contained herein.

All rights reserved. In accordance with the U.S. Copyright Act of 1976, no part of this publication may be reproduced, distributed, or transmitted in any form or by any means, or stored in a database or retrieval system, without prior written permission of the publisher, Written Dreams Publishing, Green Bay, Wisconsin 54311. Please be aware that if you've received this book with a "stripped" off cover, please know that the publisher and the author may not have received payment for this book, and that it has been reported as stolen property. Please visit www.writtendreams.com to see more of the unique books published by Written Dreams Publishing.

Publishing Editor: Brittiany Koren
Copy-editor: Samantha Koren
Illustrator: Amanda Dix
Cover Art Designer: Sunny Fassbender
Interior Layout Designer: Amanda Dix

Category: Poetry and Short Prose
Description: *A collection of poems and short stories about being a woman in all stages of life.*
Paperback ISBN: 978-1-951375-07-2
Ebook ISBN: 978-1-951375-08-9
LOCN: Catalog info applied for.
First Edition published by Written Dreams Publishing in September, 2019.

Green Bay, WI 54311

Praise for *Under the Shade of the Banyan Tree*

"Rao amazes yet again with a true sense of what the modern woman goes through every day. We must battle cultural norms yet rebel in a way to gain our wings to do what we yearn to accomplish. She describes the dual roles of women, no matter where one comes from."
—Sonali Dhir, Advance Practice Nurse, Family Nurse Practitioner

"Simi K. Rao's *Under the Shade of the Banyan Tree* is a compelling collection of poems and short stories. Dr. Rao writes with keen insight about life, love, illness, war, loss, revenge and joy. Her spare and deceptively simple poetry leaves the reader with a new appreciation of our universal humanity, and her short stories will leave you wanting more."
—Marianne Novelli, M.D.

"I read Simi K Rao's *Under the Shade of the Banyan Tree* in two sittings. I simply couldn't put it down. The short stories were penned with an appreciation for the important placement of imagery, detail, and dialogue. This skill combined with likeable and formidable characters makes for an impressive read. But it is the poetry that grabbed me. Her innate propensity for unearthing our shared humanness, no matter our differences, strikes an emotional tone that allows her reader to not only relate, but to empathize. The poetry is straight up and to the point. It does not have to be interpreted or dissected to be understood. Simi is a straight shooter and certainly had an impact on this reader."
—Dallas H, Author of *Shaking the Family Tree*

"Simi K. Rao's *Under the Shade of the Banyan Tree* is an engrossing read. Each poem tells a different story which strikes a chord with the readers instantly."
—Priyasree Naskar, Student and Educator

Praise for *The Accidental Wife*

"*The Accidental Wife* is an intriguing tale of the best-laid plans gone awry but set straight by the humbling hand of destiny. A delightful novel."
—Shobhan Bantwal, Best-selling Author of *The Dowry Bride*

Praise for *Inconvenient Relations*

"In Rao's debut novel, an arranged Indian marriage sets the stage for an intimate look at the exasperating madness of love… An often intoxicating…will-they-or-won't-they tale."
—Kirkus Reviews

"Sassy desi romance—5 stars!
—Rachelle Ayala, Best-selling Author of *Michal's Window*

To Anica

"When I stopped chasing after PERFECT I found PEACE.

Life is not about achieving perfection, it's about reconciling with your imperfections."

—*Simi K. Rao*

A Preface Poem

Jenny Delos Santos

Tears came to my eyes
as I read the poems, rants and short stories
that Simi K. Rao has written.
How can one person write so much
similarity that I felt over the years.

Were we meant to meet through the
determination of our publisher,
who wanted me to write on behalf of Rao,
a person that I've never met.
Yet her words touched my inner soul.

The poem that related a lot to me was
"Me Is All I Can Be."
I've tried numerous of times to be like
someone else instead of myself,
who I insist is someone that people
totally dislike.

Yet, today people praised me
at work when they find out I'll

Simi K. Rao

be doing a talk at UH Manoa.
Stunned as I am, I realize I can
just be myself and act like no other.

Thank you, Rao, for all your words of wisdom.
I will always remember you
until the end of my time
here on earth.

Introduction

Anica Ilić McFarlane

I have known Simi K. Rao for well over a decade as a great friend. I've watched her become a wonderful mother and daughter to her family. I've known that she had many talents, but when she shared with me that she was writing a novel a few years ago, I was surprised. I had never expected Simi to have that talent.

Throughout the writing process, she shared some of her poetry with me. I was stunned with her ability to evoke a sense of knowing and understanding. Her poems spoke to me on many levels. Her words speak to the soul. They evoke a feeling of understanding and resonance.

In her collection, *Under the Shade of the Banyan Tree*, Simi covers many subjects; everything from mundane everyday routine such as getting your child ready for school to gut-wrenching moments such as loneliness, addiction, death, and what comes after.

Poems such as "Silent Scream" arouse a visceral reaction: "yes, I have felt like this." She understands and speaks for us all. As a reader, I'm looking forward to seeing many more works from Simi K. Rao.

Under the Shade of the Banyan Tree

Gods recline and meditate
Yogis attain nirvana
Banias conduct business
Councils assemble and confer

I stand firm, yet I walk
My arms stretch across the universe,
forever seeking and growing
I am exceptional

Under the Shade of the Banyan Tree

Creatures frisk on my limbs
The weary traveler finds repose
I am a temple of benevolence
An infinite ocean of knowledge

I was there before you were born
I shall remain after you are gone
I have weathered a million storms
I am the eternal tree

About the poem: The term 'Banyan' was coined by the British after the word 'bania' who are people belonging to the trading community. Found in nearly every Indian village, the tree is the center of activity. People gather, traveling merchants of all kinds set up shop under its vast canopy, and village councils hold hearings. It is also called *Kalpavriksha*, the tree that fulfills wishes and material desires and is greatly revered. Its ability to survive and grow for centuries is akin to God providing shelter to his devotees. Its ability to send down aerial roots which grow down into the soil and form additional trunks makes it a symbol of immortality. The leaves, bark and seeds are used for various medicinal purposes. The tree is truly extraordinary.

Delirium

My words
assorted images
evanescent squiggly lines,
stumbling out of my head
in fractured sentences
Traveling in a split second
from sunny blue skies
to a cold dark room
Opening doors
with the wrong key
Standing up to put my socks on
Momentary mood swings
of visions I see
and sometimes not

Loneliness

Introducing Loneliness,
your constant companion
You lie if you say you don't know me
I'm the one who sits beside you in the empty passenger seat
I'm the stranger who smiles at you at the mall
I'm the blanket you wrap yourself in every night
I'm the clock you hear ticking in the hall
I'm the breeze that ruffles your hair on a cold winter morning
I'm the scream that reverberates through your lonely frame
I'm the earth who cradles you in the grave
Where would you be without me?

Woman

From time immemorial
this has been a woman's lot
that a man is more equal than she
history has not forgot

She toiled with him everyday
made sure he was fed
going sometimes without
none would care if she were dead

She bore him sons,
despite incredible pain

Under the Shade of the Banyan Tree

her daughters he rejected
because they brought him shame

He covered her up from head to toe
treated her like a possession
shackled her up in his house
scourged her for his own indiscretions

Would you find people more of a hypocrite
in any other part of the world
who deify innumerable goddesses
yet smother a baby girl?

Mother

The disasters and pitfalls
seem trivial
when I look at myself
through your eyes
the fragrance of innocence
lingers strong in your arms
life looks almost bearable

Silent Scream

Expanding inside
like a mushroom cloud
pouring out of my mouth,
my ears, my eyes, my skin
I choke
I scream
Let me speak

Life an Ugly Cousin

It wasn't love
that I thought I felt
but a delusion
of a needy mind

Like a monotonous ritual
I cry again
Invisible in my sorrow
tears in the rain

I long
I crave to collapse
to dissolve in my unhappiness
It just won't happen

At times like these,
death sounds sublime
a beautiful thing
and life an ugly cousin

On Edge

I purge my mind with music
I rejoice in the space
until the creatures cruise back in
on roller skates

Unbelievable

I am
Abnormal
Unconventional
Abominable
Unafraid
Aberrant
Unapologetic
Absurd
Uncommon
Absent
Undeterred
Abrasive
Unique
I am
Unbelievable

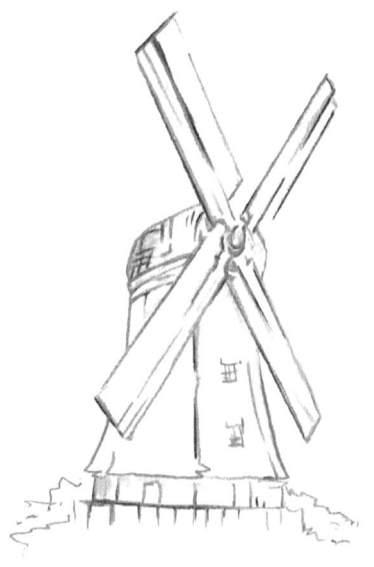

Windmills of My Mind

Sometimes up
Sometimes down
Sometimes bright
Sometimes brown

Sometimes dubious
Sometimes trusting
Sometimes active

Simi K. Rao

Sometimes resting

Laughably stupid
Brilliantly keen
Deeply perceptive
Ruthlessly mean

Shifting sands
of transitory thoughts
Windfall of emotions
tied up in knots

A waffling chameleon
A steady machine
A virulent tornado
A meandering stream

A beautiful maiden
A nasty dream
A sensitive bitch
A stoic queen

The windmills
rotate perpetually
blurring the boundaries
between illusion and reality

The Stranger

It's relentless
Oppressive
Stifling
It gets into my skull
and chokes my brain
The sand makes me blind
My mother is dead
and I feel nothing

The water offers a momentary lull
Do you love me, she asks
Yes, I want to say
but the heat has murdered my heart
I stand in the balcony
and stare at the street
What are you doing here
white man in a strange land

About the poem: This poem was inspired by the novel, ***The Stranger*** by Albert Camus. It is one of my favorite books. I was taken with it almost right away since I connected so well with the protagonist; in particular, his indifference and malaise which usually sparks a feeling of guilt in me. It calmed me to think that such people do exist.

War

The sirens begin to wail
We know the drill
We run through the streets
as the birds of prey
swoop down from the sky
We huddle in the shelter,
children and adults alike
A brood of fear
waiting for the inevitable
through the drag of time
We must repent
for the sins of our masters.

The Girl in the Window
PART 1

Her:

The world passes by
while she remains static
finding relief from her reminiscences,
Her morose thoughts

A young man walks by
an inquisitive light in his eyes
She knows not his name,
it is but a trifling detail

She welcomes the anonymous exchanges
a smile,
sometimes a wave
and conjures a hazy dream
of carefree tomorrows
and hopeful todays

The Girl in the Window
Part 2

Him:

I see her everyday
at the window of her house
Her face lurking in the shadows
finding cover in a veil of secrecy
obscurity in a shroud of seclusion
But her beauty is not hidden from me

She's a princess
from a faraway land
I know not her name
Yet she has become a part of me
My daily scenery
I miss her now that she is gone

Tyrant

As the royal backside settles on the throne
the tentacles sink into the ground
to hold and support,
to spread and choke
the length and breadth of the kingdom

The Lone Koi

I'm strong
I'm courageous
I prosper
I'm ambitious
Follow me,
I am the mistress of my own destiny.

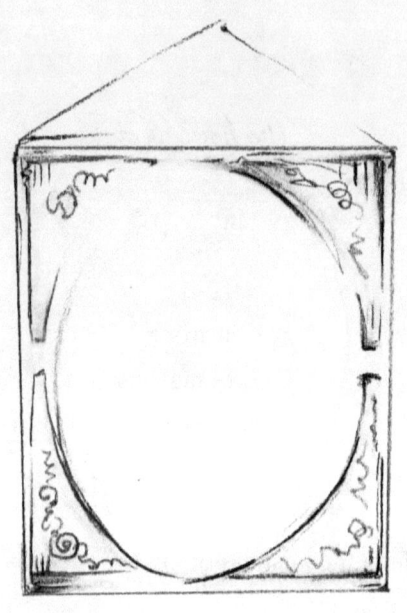

Dad

A picture hangs in my room
I have to twist my head to see it.
It's old
Can't tell how many years have passed

Memories are so fickle
They fade quicker the rawer they are

Under the Shade of the Banyan Tree

How will I remember him?
By those dreadful final moments?
Or by his smile?
I snap a picture of the photograph and send it to myself
I trace his profile with a finger.
Will you remember me when I'm gone?
Or will I fade away
like a picture on the wall.

Me Is All I Can Be

I try my best
to talk the talk, walk the walk
But I fail miserably
Who am I trying to be?

I strive to be
the best of the best
I fall, lie bruised and battered
When will I be free?

I paint myself
like a rainbow
But end up
like a fool

I work hard
to be what I can never be
So, to save me some trouble
I better just be me.

Walk on the Beach

As the orange orb gambols with the horizon
the heavens put on a dazzling display
Swiftly the embers fade
the big deep takes over
with its hypnotic cadence
Louder, louder!
The joyous wind unshackles my hair
I gulp in the sea
Gently, quickly
it delivers me to sleep.

The Bashful Bride

She sits on the rose strewn bed
a bashful bride
in all her jeweled splendor,
hennaed hands resting on drawn up knees
innocent and uninitiated,
she awaits the approach of her beloved

Crush

AN EXCERPT ORIGINALLY PUBLISHED IN SIMI K. RAO'S NOVEL, *INCONVENIENT RELATIONS*

It was a lovely dream, the loveliest she'd ever had. It had to be a dream, for how else could something so wonderful be true?

The occasion was the annual quiz contest and Maya had been chosen to represent their high school as the most likely candidate to win back the coveted trophy they had so narrowly lost to Mt. Carmel last year. Everyone was sure she was the only one who could do it. Not just everyone, she was, too, because she always won everything. She was invincible.

Maya was oozing with confidence, egged on by the looks of nervous despair on the opposing team members' faces (her reputation had preceded her) and the shouts and hoots of encouragement and cheer from her own school mates who had turned out in droves. The battle lines were drawn, and she had been crowned the indisputable queen.

That is until she saw him, and he saw her.

Her mind—needle sharp, ever alert intellect went blank and the rest of her came alive. It was as though she had been struck by a lightning bolt, though she'd never had the experience, but the sensation couldn't be equated with anything else she'd been through.

He was the Quiz master, new that year and replacing

the old one, who with his sonorous voice and pompous attitude had become passe and an object of ridicule. Young, handsome, dynamic and self-assured—her ideal male counterpart, a person she believed didn't exist.

Maya was thrown off her moorings. Try as hard as she could, it proved impossible to wrench him off her sphere of vision.

So, it appeared was his lot as well. Even while posing questions to others, she seemed to remain his sole object of interest. When it was her turn—every single time—her responses would freeze in her throat and she could do nothing but stare blankly back at him like a mute numbskull.

Was it love at first sight? No, that was silly adolescent crap. It was more than that. It was desire, a raw naked primal want she recognized in those brazen eyes that caused her body to shiver and the heat to rise to her cheeks. That was it. She was done for. He had stolen her thunder and she'd been dethroned even before the coronation.

The cheers turned into boos as her school lost again, and this time, by an unheard of margin. She left the stage acutely embarrassed, but what pained her even more was a deep yearning that would remain unfulfilled.

It was a lonely trip home. Somewhere along the way she was accosted and jostled into a dark alley. She was trapped in a rough yet sensual embrace. A pair of hands roamed her nubile body in such a familiar manner that her knees turned to water. She would have collapsed to the ground had she not been held up.

Turning her around, he ventured a simple question, "Will you run away with me?"

She scored with her answer. "Yes."

Love Is...

Love is innocent
It is pure
It is tough
It can endure

Love is like a rock
it stands the test of time
Love is tender
A sweet surrender

Love is honey
that can taste bitter
It is desire
Sets hearts a flutter

Love is hardship
It may take years to master
A genuine exertion
may resolve this puzzler

Simi K. Rao

Love is bizarre
Tough to fathom
It is a riddle
An eternal convolution

Love is fatal
most fall victim
Remedies are simple
a look, a touch, a dimple.

I Am Nothing

I look in the mirror
What do I see
An empty skull
hidden under a layer of flesh and blood
I am nothing
but a bunch of chemical formulas

If I pass tomorrow
I'll be mourned a short time
then forgotten
like a wound that heals, leaving no scar behind
Life begins and ends
no two opinions about it

Then why
do I worry and fret?
do I smile, nod and fake empathy?
do I chase after depression?

Simi K. Rao

I am a grain of sand on the beach
A drop in the ocean
A speck of dust in a largely unknown universe
A fraction of a second on the clock of life
I am nothing.

Windows

Clean, plain, open, closed, bright,
light, shaded, paned, shuttered, blinded, boarded,
rusty, dirty, smoky windows.
broken, shattered, run down windows
Windows that protect and hide,
a mirror to the world outside
and sometimes to the world within,
unraveling layer by layer, revealing
a glance into a soul,
a tool for introspection and scrutiny,
secrets and smokescreens,
evasions, denials, half-truths
Windows, they tell it all.

Coward

My hands freeze
on the wheel
Horns scorn,
they fly around,
they tease
I'm weary
of the constant conflict
of picking up the gauntlet
of being a 'MAN'
Go on, heckle me
I don't care
I am a coward

White Room

I lie on the bed
in the white room.
They sit around me,
these strangers with familiar voices.
I think we are waiting for something
or someone.
These strangers, they look at me.
They mutter words I don't understand.
A man in a white coat walks in.
He stands next to my bed.
He speaks not to me,
but to these strangers.
They are talking about me, I know.
About what, I don't understand.
Irritated, I kick off the covers.
Mother! They chide me and pull them back.

Simi K. Rao

About the poem: This is a poem about dementia, the hallmark of the disease being loss of memory. I write about a scene I came across during my rounds in the hospital—an elderly woman in the advanced stages of dementia is lying on the bed surrounded by her caring relatives. It's difficult to know what's going on in the poor woman's mind because she has lost the ability to speak, even comprehend. Yet it's apparent she's unaware of her ailment. She doesn't even know where she is or who she is with.

My Day

As I walk along these corridors
enveloped by disease and disinfectant,
I become a part of the scenery,
invisible in my white coat

I'm a stranger,
who begets instant trust.
I see you at your worst—
you bare all to me

Life passes
Another is born
Hope is still alive
After every night, there is morn.

Changes

Yesterday I met a young man in the hospital. I had seen him before, maybe a few months ago. He had an odd name, a name you don't expect to forget easily, but I did somehow. I must be getting old, I think.

His name didn't strike a bell when the ER doc told me about him, but I remembered his face.

"He's a nice guy;" the ER doc said. "He really is," he reiterated.

That had me curious. We don't speak like that often. We physicians are a cynical bunch, you see.

I recognized the young man right away, and it was a shock. He didn't look at all like he had just a month or so ago. He had shrunk. Literally deflated by several pounds and he had grown a beard to disguise his gaunt face.

He had been a young man in the prime of his life. Big, muscular, strong. Still hopeful and smiling, even after a heart attack at thirty-two. Still hopeful and smoking.

He was still smiling now, but it was a different kind of smile. There was diffidence in it and fear and uncertainty. There was also hope, but it was fading fast. It's astounding how clearly I perceived it without him having to say a word.

Instinctively, I clasped his hand. It was perhaps the most spontaneous thing I've done. It was the best way I could express myself other than crying for this man's life.

That'd be a terrible thing to do.

He had given up smoking after the surgery. Ever since they told him he had cancer. We talked some more. I explained why he was here. The spots in his lungs could be pneumonia.

"Maybe they are," he said and smiled. He'd become adept at dealing with bad news. He had aged beyond his years in such a short time. My heart wept for him.

How Long

How long can I fight
How much can I hope
How long can I wait for life to take a turn
How much can I stretch the rope
How long can I scream inside
How much more can I cope?

Carnival of Life

As the earth spins
and time rolls on,
affection becomes an obligation.

Lines deepen into wrinkles,
the present becomes the past,
and the past, history.

As the weary spine sags to embrace the ground,
the carnival of life stops for no one—
it simply goes on.

Lone Cloud

A lofty sojourn
A solitary quest
to territories unknown
through fields of unrest

Like a fragile dream
an evanescent memory
I fumble on
another precarious journey

Mr. Tim

"Alyeeee…!"

Mom's voice whizzed past my six-year-old ears before the morning sun swallowed it up like it does everything else—the moon, the stars. Dreams. I didn't yell back a response. I had better things to do.

I was in the backyard, standing barefoot on the wet grass. I love the grass. I love the way it catches the sun in the morning and how it crunches under my feet and bounces right back up after I've stomped on it with all my might. But that happens to be my second favorite memory. My first is Mr. Tim.

Mr. Tim was my friend. My secret friend (you know how little kids like to have secret friends). We first met behind the giant old beech tree. No one liked to go near it, but I did. Big trees don't scare me.

It was springtime. I know because I could smell the lilacs and the leaves were the color of freshly squeezed lemonade. The faded deck above me creaked like Nana's old knees as I eyed the steep slope. Then, like always, I ran-skipped a few steps, then dropped and slid the rest of the way on my bottom. It was so fun, even though I knew later Mom would give me ten with her wooden spoon.

I slapped at my jammies to get rid of the mud and twigs, then stood up and hugged the tree. I slid slowly around it, making loud squelching sounds as my feet sank into the ground, soggy from the sprinklers Dad had left running late into the night. I giggled when the tree scratched my face as my fingers dug into the holes in its trunk. Someone had carved his name on it. Someone I didn't know. L-I-O-N-E-L. Another secret. I giggled louder.

Hush! Mr. Tim is here!

I looked up and saw him watching me from way up high in the branches. His big bushy tail wiggled and snapped, up and down, side to side then stayed quiet. I spotted something red in his hands. We had a long staring match. I didn't give up even when my neck began to hurt. Then he was gone in a flash.

He came back the next day. I decided he liked me. I offered him some peanuts that I had snuck from Dad's stash. Dad liked to gorge on them while watching TV. He would scatter the shells all over the carpet, even though Mom made him clean up afterwards.

Mr. Tim liked the peanuts very much. He snatched them from my hand and jumped right back up into the tree, scurrying up the trunk in a flash. Then he came down for more. The following week he let me pat his little head with my finger while he ate.

I tried to follow him up the tree, but I couldn't. I would slide down to the ground each time and scrape my knees. I think he figured that out because he came down to the ground and let me chase him around. He ran, hopped, jumped and flew. Yes, he did. Like a bird.

Then one day he didn't come. I waited and waited. Mom said maybe he forgot (you see she'd discovered my secret). But when she saw my face scrunch up, she said, "Maybe he found a new friend, Aly, and a new tree. Squirrels are like that. Don't fret."

But Mr. Tim didn't forget, nor did he go anywhere else. I found him under some leaves behind the tree. He had kept his promise. It was I who had been late.

I must have cried an ocean that day.

Me and I
(A Conspiracy Theory)

When I stumbled into me
a weirder thing couldn't be.

We are but one and the same,
yet go by different names.

We share the same vessel,
yet forever tussle
like a gargoyle in my suitcase.

A stranger in the mirror
meets me at every corner,
throwing me in a quandary.

Am I I?
Or am I me?

Sometimes You Need To...

Zap your brain
Be honest
Skip the small talk
Burn your house
Strip naked
Love your reflection
Drive without headlights
Scrub your face
Stare at the sun
Get lost in the rain.

Passing

Death is…
An irreversible end
A period
A fearful realm
A mysterious unknown

A culmination of sins
An inescapable truth
An unbreakable bond
An endless repose

Therefore,
just hold my hand
Give me fortitude
to make the journey
when my heart has run its course.

Addiction

Paper skin tents under my fingers
I stare into her yellow eyes
What's your name?
Jane, she says.
Do you know where you are?
A blank look,
followed by an edentulous smile
I think I had too much to drink, she explains.

I hunt for her pulse
Her belly is a giant rubber ball
Indignation rushes to my head
and out my mouth
Why? I ask.
She shrugs her bony shoulders
and starts to cry.
I couldn't help it, she whispers.

Under the Shade of the Banyan Tree

About the poem: This poem is about a woman whose liver had failed due to her addiction. She was an alcoholic. She managed to get on the transplant list after remaining sober for several months (a requirement). But she started to drink again, and her excuse was that her only support, her mother, had killed herself. These are the moments when I find myself in a terrible bind. I couldn't do much for her beyond holding her hand.

Growing Pains

Tiny fingers clutching tight
won't let go
Moist gurgles of joy
Eyes shining with recognition
Giggles that fill my ears with bliss

The in-between years
The present continuous
The confused interim
They zip past
faster than I can breathe

Now tall, shooting up like a reed
in front of my astonished eyes
Absent smiles
Hugs not so mutual
The clings, I miss them so

Soon she'll be gone
Adrift
into a big, wide wicked world

Under the Shade of the Banyan Tree

and she won't look back
Though I sincerely hope she'll know
How much I love her

Mom, I get you now

The Surface

We operate
You and I
We nod, we converse, we agree
We go about our business
On the surface

The chinks
They show on occasion
We conceal them
expertly shroud them
On the surface

Those who dare
peep beneath
rear aghast
at the ugliness they see
They return promptly
to the surface

A cauldron of noxious brews
Voices falling on deaf ears

Under the Shade of the Banyan Tree

Conflicting emotions
Forgotten affections
Trivialized relations
Broken promises

Still, all appears just fine
On the surface

Butterfly

My heart is a butterfly
drifting aimless in the breeze
floating without a care
Fluttering my wings
of resplendent silk
and lustrous

You lay eyes upon me
and watch in wonder
As I dance
in a trance
To the song of freedom
and the music of love

A Seed of Doubt

Once you encounter
the seed of doubt
It is tough
to get it out

It starts to flourish,
spread its roots
It feeds itself,
sprouts new shoots

It manipulates the mind
poisons the soul
What you hear, see or say
isn't under your control

The longer you procrastinate,
the stronger the affliction
Soon there will be no remedy
from this evil addiction

Simi K. Rao

The only antidote, if any
is to sow the seed of trust
Nurture it with loving care
and guard it you must.

Get Out

Get out
Take a walk
Let the birds do the talking

A River

POEM ORIGINALLY PUBLISHED IN SIMI K. RAO'S NOVEL, ***INCONVENIENT RELATIONS***

Meandering eternal

Perennial
over mile and mile
of barren desert,
golden field,
rugged canyon

From a faint trickle to
a booming roar
It contorts, twists, rushes
and flows
its mood ever changing.

From a pensive calm
to a nurturing warmth
and a restless fury

Under the Shade of the Banyan Tree

in constant motion
a persistent quest
to its ocean
where its spirit can rest

Liberty

I have everything
Freedom to speak, to choose, to love

Still, I'm trapped
in a closet of noise, worry, anxiety
and perception

My wrinkles
My lack of beauty
My aging mind
My cancer

An acknowledgment for
the ordinariness that remains

I need liberty
away from my big house and smart kid
From the constant urge to scale a summitless peak
From fatigue

Under the Shade of the Banyan Tree

> I need detachment
> not from the world,
> But from me, myself
> I need peace.

The Good Earth

Don't look at me
O cruel accursed sun
Man-god of the sky
Don't mock me with your brilliance
You bake the earth
You lay cracks upon it
You tear it apart
You killed my mother
You gave me an illusion of plenty,
then you made me starve
You gave me a good woman,
who tilled my land with me
Then you snatched her away
You stole my innocence
You fed me greed and lust
You drained my heart
You took my life

Under the Shade of the Banyan Tree

About the poem: This poem was inspired by the novel, ***The Good Earth*** by Pearl S. Buck. Ms. Buck's masterpiece classic tells the story of Wang Lung, a poor farmer in pre-revolution China. My poem is a metaphor that depicts the intense and intimate connection between man and his land and how any changes in it are carried over into his personal life.

The Stench of Fear

Wild beasts roar
The galleries erupt,
baying for blood
The stench of fear
The whites of eyes
The ruthlessness of mankind
History repeats itself everyday
What has changed?
The methods of sin.

Free

Vast forever vistas
Solitudes sublime
Feet that wander
Dreams that climb
To reach untenable heights
Unchained
Unbound
Free

Crossfire

Like a random bird in the sky
I fall
senseless
I meld with the dust
of another land
I remain nameless
Who am I?
But another random bird in the sky

About the poem: This poem is about the Malaysian passenger flight 17 that was shot down on July 17, 2014 when it flew over a war zone. It is about innocents getting caught in the crossfire.

Voyeurs

Voyeurs, we are all
unrepentant, peeping toms
Stripped, benumbed
Staring dispassionate
at the world at large
while our souls rot inside

Words

Words are bland
unless spiced with emotion

Prayer means less
unless said with devotion

Love is an empty pot
unless filled with trust

Earth is a barren spot
without its green crust

History is a blank slate
without old tales to tell

Heavens wouldn't be in demand
without the ill repute of hell

Smile

Spontaneous
Instantaneous
No instruction required
When it reaches the eyes,
it spreads like the flu
Contagious
Infectious
The universal language of a smile

Little Miss Sunshine

Grumpy
after a long night
Battling an irresistible instinct
to nod on the wheel
or run through the red light

I can't hit the sack
Not yet
It's Friday still

School drop
Chores
Endless chores

Under the Shade of the Banyan Tree

Milk's run out
and yes, apples, too
Can't do without those apples.

I prowl around
in a half daze
Dumping stuff
in my recyclable cloth bag
Green is my middle name

Disaster strikes
at the checkout counter
All my effects on the floor
displayed for the world
to see and ridicule

And just when I'm ready
to pitch and scram
before tears sprout
I sense
a gentle tap on the arm

The grocery clerk
A warm smile on her face
An implicit understanding
Everything will be fine
because of Ms. Sunshine

Phobia

Fear subjugates
Mind imprisons
Freedom loiters
In the periphery
Just out of reach

In Moderation

Don't drink
If you do,
drink in Moderation

Play
But if you are a player,
play in Moderation

Eat to live
But if you have a sweet tooth,
consume in moderation

Enjoy life
But don't go overboard,
live in Moderation

Give
But keep some for yourself,
donate in moderation

Simi K. Rao

Speak
But not before you think,
talk in moderation

Help
But don't go bankrupt,
be generous in moderation

Look good
But not too good,
look good in moderation

Be an individual
But embrace differences,
differ in moderation

Love
But don't be obsessive,
love in moderation

Make friends
But don't trust everyone,
be friendly in moderation

Hypocrite

I'm envious of those
who speak their minds
without fear of judgment.

I wish for inebriation,
for the influence of drink
so I can bare my soul, too.
You see, I am a hypocrite.

Jaded

Being me
Happy in my own skin
No hang ups,
or stress of fitting in

No designer labels
or affected talk

No painted face
or a stumbling stiletto walk

Just me in my faded jeans
My very own style
My ugly face
and my jaded smile

October

Misty drifts in the morning
A sunny chill in the air
Outside the window
lies an endless rainbow

The bough snaps back
the harvest tumbles to the ground
I lie on the grass,
drunk in the dreamy afternoon

While the little critters prepare for bed
and the goblins come out to play
The earth queen rides by,
glorious in her flamboyant train

Exotic Places

Along ancient streets
and by-lanes,
alien sounds ebb and flow

With familiar inflections
passions don't simmer,
they explode

Stirring smiles
on drab countenances
The air vibrates with soul

The Witching Hour

I watched the dense thicket of clouds slide over the giant luminous cookie in the sky. A pitch-black darkness descended over the neighborhood, and there was not a single streetlamp to mar it.

It appeared that All Saints Eve was going to live up to its reputation after all. I glanced at my companion. I could

Under the Shade of the Banyan Tree

tell she was thinking the same.

"Should we start? The time looks right," Myra said.

"Yeah, let's go." I smiled at my long-time friend and neighbor.

She adjusted her lace-up corset and handed me her long and tattered train before gingerly stepping out of the alley that had been our hideout ever since the beginning of our ritual. Once again, I had to pause to admire her elaborate costume. She was pleased with it, especially since she had put it together herself. The delicate tea-stained ivory lace and tulle dress accented with droopy brown roses gave her a wispy and forlorn look. The many years of our adventures had supplied a precious aura of authenticity to the dress, as it had been tripped on and ripped several times.

Slowly, we made our way through the familiar streets we fondly called our haunt. They had watched us grow from carefree children into not very responsible young adults. We had roamed these alleys innumerable times, even in our dreams. Being here made us feel at home.

For a moment, I stood still and closed my eyes. The night air was flavored with moist earth and pumpkin spice crumble. I gulped it down hungrily.

Tonight, as always, silence was the key, broken only by the rustle of the rotting leaves that swept the sidewalk.

We listened, mesmerized. Five long years had gone by, but to me, it seemed like yesterday.

Suddenly, the wind came rushing by our feet. It gathered up the leaves and they danced and twirled in the middle of the street.

"Brrrr...it's cold." Myra laughed, and I joined her. It was close to freezing and neither of us had jackets on.

"Let's walk faster," I said.

The houses stood out like cardboard cutouts against the inky black sky. Most of them had some kind of décor, except Mr. Blacksmith's—or Mr. Blackheart—as we used to call him as children. Ever since he had moved in more than ten years ago, not once had he turned on his lights or handed out candy.

The Millers, on the other hand, had gotten more and more flamboyant with each passing year. What had begun with a few pumpkins and a cobweb screen on the porch had now turned into an ambitious graveyard project. Tombstones could be seen everywhere with rotting carcasses spilling out of the ground. A zombie undertaker dug his own grave while a phantom funeral procession made its final journey under the watch of a flock of rapacious ravens.

"Halloween is my favorite time of the year. It has an attitude all its own; people using their imagination to be someone entirely different makes it both enchanting and spooky," I said.

I had always wanted to dress up as a matador, don a magnificent bolero jacket, and swing my satin cape at the imaginary bull.

"But we can't change our look now," Myra admonished me.

It was a wonder how well she read my mind. We could have been twins.

I nodded. It was a bummer. We had given each other our word to keep the same getup we had on that fateful night five years ago.

Myra squeezed my hand. "At least it happened on Halloween." She couldn't have been more right.

We hung back to allow a couple of kids to run ahead, their parents staying close behind. We were good, well-behaved teens. And we weren't really out for candy. It was something else that drew us together tonight.

A group of fine little elves skipped by. "The costumes seem to be getting better every year."

Myra nodded, looking at a little girl with glow-in-the-dark wings and a light up necklace. She was out alone

Under the Shade of the Banyan Tree

with an adult, probably her father. She tugged at his sleeve, appearing to seek his permission before bounding up a driveway. We saw her skip around a grinning Jack O' lantern, then come to a hesitant stop on the porch. The door had opened on its own and out of the yawning darkness slid out a most unusual creature consisting of a large grotesque green face and spindly white hands. The little girl turned around and ran back, screaming to her dad.

A young family had a huge lab in tow. He shrunk back and whined when he saw us. Then, when he thought we'd retreated a safe distance, he began to bark.

Myra and I broke out into giggles. This was turning out to be real fun.

There was a party going on in the next street. A loud one. We choose to skip it. The shortcut back passed us through a secluded copse. I caught my arm in the underbrush and ripped my sleeve. "Our costumes are getting old!" I whined.

"But isn't that the idea?" my friend said, putting her arm through mine. The slash on her forehead and the festering wound on her left shoulder couldn't have looked more real.

We'd walked quite a ways and Myra was beginning to look restless. I glanced at the cracked face of my dollar store watch.

"Hey, have we seen you two before?"

I looked up.

A couple of boys had appeared out of nowhere. One tall, the other short and rotund. They looked like high schoolers. Sophomores or seniors, it was hard to make out.

Myra and I looked at each other. "Maybe…" I said, trying to sound mysterious.

Myra's hold tightened on my arm.

We turned around and started walking again. The

houses disappeared. The road changed from pavement to loose gravel. We picked up our pace. The boys followed. We still looked good, despite our costumes.

After some time, we approached a long, white-washed picket fence that shone eerily in the moonlight. Beyond it was a stretch of tall sparkling grass. A grey fog hung suspended over it. A dense black forest could be seen on the other side.

I clambered over, and my practiced fingers found the hidden latch. The gate groaned open and Myra floated in like a queen.

"Hey, where are you going?" one of the boys asked.

"A place you've never been before." Myra suggested coyly, standing in the middle of the meadow.

The squat boy who was dressed like a pirate burst into a high-pitched giggle. "Hey, this is cool!"

I glanced at his quieter, better looking pal. He reminded me of someone I used to know.

"What are you waiting for? Afraid of an adventure?" I asked, holding the gate open.

He snapped up the bait and rushed in, his mate following close behind.

I shut the gate. It was always easier when there was more than one.

* * *

At ninety-eight going on ninety-nine, Mrs. Maybelle Merriwether was one of the oldest continuous residents of Hazardville, a small township in Kentucky. She had her own house with a large sprawling ranch near the edge of town. She had lived there alone after the passing of her beloved husband of sixty-five years, except for a maid

Under the Shade of the Banyan Tree

who came twice a week. None of her well-wishers had been able to persuade her to move.

"Memories," she told them. "I live for my memories. This old house has almost all of them."

But it wasn't as if she was out of touch with current affairs. She was an authority when it came to information regarding her beloved town. The residents and regular visitors to the town knew to be on the lookout for the little old woman who sat on her porch everyday sipping tea and scouring the local newspaper cover to cover.

Today was November 2, 1996. It was a special day because Mrs. Merriwether was in a hurry. She did not wait to set her kettle to boil before picking up her copy of *The Hazardville Enterprise* that someone had thoughtfully slid inside the mailbox attached to the front door. She quickly found what she was looking for. Tucked at the bottom of the third page were two advertisements titled 'Missing'.

She had to sit down and take a few breaths to calm the fluttering of her heart before reading further. Both the ads were fairly similar. Two young men, they said; Nathan Pierce, 17, and Diego Sanchez, 18, both seniors at Hazardville High, had been reported missing since the night of Halloween. Nathan was dressed as a cowboy while Diego was wearing a pirate costume. They had attended a party at a mutual friend's house and had left slightly before midnight, saying they were going for a walk. They were last seen on Rushmore street near Old Mill Road.

Mrs. Merriwether leaned back in her chair and closed her eyes. Old Mill Road led to a large marshland that encircled Silver Moon Lake. Most of the lake had been drained to accommodate the expanding town population, but a large expanse of it still remained. Over time, several people had drowned there. The town chamber had elected to have cordoned off all access points and put up huge signs warning everyone to *keep off*.

Yet, for the past four years on Halloween, high school boys had gone missing from the very same spot. Their bodies were never found. They had simply disappeared without a trace.

Five years ago, two young girls out trick or treating had been fatally run over by drunk high schoolers near the area. Mrs. Merriwether had always wondered if that was a coincidence. Now, she wasn't so sure.

Halloween

There are some who await
the call of the moon
Who stalk amongst us
reckless and brazen
Beware of the beast

Simi K. Rao

Rooftops

Beautiful asymmetry
Stucco walls
tiled red
Undulating crevices
Gutters that conceal
while cracks reveal
Murky pasts
Broken dreams
Caged hearts
Upended lives
that hide in the shadows
and seek sanctuary beneath
these rooftops

Winter

A beauty; stark, harsh, and pure
Drab world of grey, black, and white
Naked bodies lie abandoned and cold

Fluffy balls of cotton
suspended from dormant limbs
Yonder forth towering peaks
defined pristine
Shoulders huddle

Simi K. Rao

against air frigid, sharp, and crisp
while the hope of warmth
frisks among the clouds

Mundane

We run around everyday
busying ourselves in a mundane routine
Getting the kids off to school
soccer practice, summer camp
Going to work, returning home, working again
making dinner, walking the dog, feeding the cat
Worrying about the future, finances
And the cycle repeats

We dread to stop and think
beyond the mundaneness
We continue like busy little ants until
someone steps on us with a giant shoe
and life is over as we know it

If we survive, we become philosophers
to dispense mundane wisdom
that no one cares to heed
as they are busy, too, living their own mundane lives.

Red

Pure
Desirable
Auspicious
Fertile
Woman
Unclean
Untouchable
Accursed
Exile

About the poem: The color *red* is so much a part of a woman's life, as it is also a curse. It's associated with many things: at the minimum, discomfort—to shame, impurity, banishment, segregation. It's also a commanding color, and women have embraced it to make a powerful statement about themselves.

The Ritual

It happened at one of the five-star hotels, Marriott I think, the fancy one in Juhu. Thank heavens it wasn't at his home.

The room was cavernous and daunting, with creepy shadows all over created by the hidden lighting everyone is so crazy about nowadays. I was led in by two of my new husband's giggly cousins. I'd have loved to smack their pretty faces, but that'd have invited a huge ruckus. Besides, I was preoccupied.

I was terrified. Terrified of doing it with someone I didn't know anything about. What little I did know could be googled on the web. But then, was my lot different from most other women? Examples were all around me—my mom, my aunts, cousins, and friends.

Maybe it was because everything had happened so fast; because I had no clue of the future; because the ghost of Rohan still clung to me like my own shadow. Because. Because. Because…

The elaborately made up bed; the cloying scent of jasmine; the milk on the nightstand—it all sent me into a state of panic.

I felt sick.

We Indians talk so much about *sanskars* and morality and then a single ritual authorizes sex between perfect strangers. Madness!

I was desperate to make a run for it. But my Indianness—my culture—held me back. The scenes from the aftermath played in my mind. People searching all over for me. The terrible shame. I didn't really care. But my parents would. Besides, where would I go? No lover was waiting for me with open arms.

It was depressing, but not worth dwelling on. I was, am a practical woman.

I spied my overnight bag set discreetly in a corner. Someone had been thoughtful enough to bring it in for me. I yanked at my jewelry, not caring when it caught on the fabric of my neon pink brocade saree. I quickly changed into the new red silk nightie I had bought on an impulse a couple of weeks ago. I don't know what had prompted me to do so. It all seemed so silly now. The fine fabric felt cool on my skin.

I took the left side of the bed as it was closest to the window. That would give me something to stare at while…I couldn't bring myself to think about what would happen next.

I lay down and was almost immediately seized by a violent shiver. Even my teeth chattered.

I tugged the cotton sheet loose and wrapped it snugly around myself and tucked it under my feet. Then I pulled the subtly perfumed heavy patchwork quilt on top. Maybe it was the weight or the warmth, but it helped me calm down.

I was about to drift off to sleep when I heard the door click open behind me, followed by the sound of creaky, new leather sandals. The muffled sound of running water in the bathroom was almost drowned out by my pulse banging in my head. I held my breath, waiting, hoping for a miracle. They say if you wish really hard for something you can make it happen.

I got the shock of my life when the bed sank under his weight. He slipped his arm around me. It was icy cold. I wrapped mine tight across my chest as he spooned my entire length with his body and nuzzled into my neck.

I squeezed my legs together and closed my eyes.

His breath smelled extra minty. He was trying too hard. "Are you asleep?"

"No," I said quietly.

His thing rubbed into my backside. I had felt one before. In the local bus, as a schoolgirl; as a teenager and a young adult, victimized by the random sexual predator. I wanted to throw up. Instead, I tried to squeeze myself tighter and sink inside.

He tried to roll me over.

I couldn't take it anymore. "Please Suraj! I don't think I'm ready yet."

It's fair to say he didn't force himself on me. For that, I was grateful.

While my disgruntled husband rolled away and slept, I stayed awake until the wee hours of the morning clinging to my side of the bed as if it was the rock that'd save me from drowning in the river I'd willingly plunged into. Ultimately, fatigue took over.

When I opened my eyes again, the sun was already riding high in the sky. And, as is usually the case, nightmares have a habit of dissipating in daylight. Had I imagined it all? I didn't think so.

Suraj was well educated, widely read, an intellectual in fact. He'd appeared rational, calm, and receptive to my opinion every time we'd met. Then why did it have to happen this way?

I figured I needed to talk to him. I saw his side of the bed empty.

Assailed with anxiety, I rushed to the door in my bedraggled state and threw it open. My new husband was lounging in the adjoining living area, his nose deep in the morning newspaper, looking businesslike in a pinstripe navy shirt and khaki pants. I vaguely recalled him informing me at our first meeting that he was a news junkie.

He glanced up and smiled, seemingly none the worse for wear. "Oh, so you're awake. Hope you slept well." He didn't wait for my reply. "Do you want to freshen up? I took the liberty of ordering breakfast, if you don't mind. I was famished."

I noticed the cart with a couple of covered dishes and two carafes. Suraj had poured himself a cup. On the coffee table was a plate with the remnants of toast on it.

The tea had grown lukewarm when I emerged some fifteen minutes later, dressed and ready for the day.

"Let me order you some hot food and tea. What'd you like, Aanchal?" Suraj said, picking up the phone.

"I'm not hungry. We need to talk."

"Sure. About what?"

"About last night…"

Suraj set the phone down and looked at me.

I cleared my throat, then went on to tell him—leaving out the graphic details—about the episodes of harassment I'd faced as a girl, then later as a young woman in medical school. They were incidents many women deal with but had left a lasting mark on me. I didn't tell him about Rohan, the man I'd fallen hopelessly in love with, who'd gone on to marry my best friend after getting her pregnant. Suraj would've probably laughed at me, or accused me of marrying him on the rebound, a fact I wouldn't have been able to deny.

He looked confused. "I get it," he said. "But Aanchal, you're a doctor. You should know about these things."

I was taken aback. "What do you mean, being a doctor I should know? Should I know about the urges a man has, no matter how old or young he may be, that he chooses not to control himself, but thrusts himself on any random woman he comes across? And he does it again and again? And the poor girl doesn't speak about it because she feels ashamed and blames herself, just like I did? Harassment is harassment, period. Nothing excuses it. It's even worse when you know the person."

It was obvious Suraj hadn't expected this kind of outburst from his brand-new wife on the first morning of his married life. For his sake, he looked suitably embarrassed.

"I shouldn't have said that. It was very insensitive of me. I don't know what I was thinking. Please, accept my sincere apologies. My behavior has been abominable. I'm sorry if I seemed in a rush or too eager last night. You happen to be a very attractive woman and I think I got carried away. I took you for granted, which I absolutely shouldn't have. I never meant to force myself on you and I never will."

The declaration was unexpected but genuine enough that I felt compelled to relent.

Suraj went on, "I really want our relationship to work. We'll take it slow, I promise. Let's get to know each other better first. We've plenty of time for everything else."

I guess that's what I was looking for—a spouse who respected my feelings. I didn't know what the future held.

Still, this was a good beginning.

Shapes of Silence

Silence light and spry
flutters like a restless bird
Compels voices to
drop to a whisper

It grows heavy
Hangs on my head
like a dead weight
crushing my spine

Then, all of a sudden
it whirls around
starts to shout
raining missiles of spite

Silence in my mind
It shrouds me in a stupor
and drags me
into darkness

A Cup of Chai

"The delivery truck was late today. Maybe you can come back in half an hour? If not, that's okay, too. I'll ask Pedro to set aside some *bhindi* and *methi,* since I know that's something you're always on the lookout for. You can also give me a list," Mrs. Shah said, making an appearance from the back of the store.

"It's alright. I can wait. I'm in no hurry." Roma smiled at the sprightly shop owner.

"As you wish." Mrs Shah turned to head back, then

hesitated. "I just received a shipment of a new tea brand from Assam, if you'd like to check it out. I know you prefer coffee, though Mr. Chattopadhyay recommends it highly."

"*Zaroor*, I will. And by the way, I *do* like tea," Roma said.

Roma wandered among the aisles of Shah Groceries located in a small suburb of Chicago. She paced herself, as there wasn't much ground to cover. Not that she needed to get anything. There were enough supplies at home to last a couple of months, if not more.

A certain nostalgia drew her to this place. A certain *desiness* that was enough to make her change two buses, walk several blocks, and navigate a busy intersection every week. It was a lovely little shop. Mrs. Shah kept the shelves well stocked with packages of snacks, pickles, dals, oils, a variety of flours, rice, and spices organized in a way they could be easily located. Roma liked to scrutinize them and read their familiar names, translated sometimes imprecisely in English. They were also meticulously displayed, unlike the other store Anand had taken her to two days ago. His excuse—the goods were priced considerably less—which was false. Roma had checked. The difference was minor. Well, perhaps not for all products, but many of them. That place had looked like a small storm had passed through it with packing cartons scattered all over the floor and the shelves overloaded and in complete disarray. Roma feared some of them may topple over, but none of the customers seemed to care. They looked intent in saving their precious cents.

She could tell Mrs. Shah took pride in her store, just like Roma's mother had in her kitchen. She could see her standing in front of the stove, dabbing her forehead with her *pallu* every now and then to keep the sweat from running into her eyes. At the same time, demonstrating an amazing amount of coordination between stirring the *chole*, rolling out precise rounds of *puris,* and frying them to perfection. Her greatest reward was when Roma cleaned her plate in record time, or so she had believed.

How naîve I've been.

She picked up a packet of cloves and held it to her nose. There wasn't even the slightest hint of the sharp, pungent aroma. How she wished Mrs. Shah had chosen to display the spices in bulk so their aroma could scent and revitalize the air rather than be confined in neat little bags of sterile plastic. Unfortunately, that was impractical, according to Mrs Shah.

"People are way too busy here. They want everything quick and easy, unlike you, my dear."

Sometimes they talked. Or rather, Mrs. Shah talked and Roma listened.

After the rush died down, she poured Roma a glass of chilled lassi and beckoned her to join her behind the counter, patting the bar stool she'd somehow managed to fit into the cramped space. The story was always the same, with details added in here and there. With each retelling, the story became more emotional as if Mrs. Shah was unravelling herself, bit by bit. She related about how she'd arrived in the States as a young bride, leaving a large family behind in the homeland. The early years had gone by pleasantly enough, though. Mr. Shah suffered a few setbacks in the business.

"You know, starting trouble, as they say back home?" Mrs. Shah said with a gentle twist of her lips. "We were young then and our dreams kept our enthusiasm alive."

Sadly, Mr. Shah caught a fatal disease. A condition that affected his nerves. "The doctors said he'd be fine. It was just an infection. But he wasn't. He lost coordination in his legs. He started to fall. Then he was in a wheelchair. In a matter of months, it became so he couldn't feed himself. He had trouble swallowing, even speaking. The doctors had to put a tube in his stomach so he wouldn't starve to death."

Mrs. Shah's voice cracked. "My Vishnu loved food. He implored me to feed him *khandvi* and *puran poli*, but I remained stern. I wonder why now. He'd have died anyway."

She paused and looked away as she relived the pain. "I'd heard of people dying like that, but I always thought they were old and frail, not strong like Vishnu. He was young, not even fifty. Imagine a robust man who worked all day long and then came home to play with his sons to become helpless like a child. He was devastated."

Mr. Shah finally passed after a long stint in the hospital. "He refused to go on a ventilator." He left behind a wife and two adolescent sons. "It was a period of horrible emptiness and fear. I'd never felt so alone before," Mrs Shah said.

Then, while Roma searched for something to say that didn't sound frivolous, a change came over her elderly companion. She straightened her spine and her voice grew strong, as if she'd received a shot of some miracle concoction.

"I didn't run back home with my tail between my legs. No, I didn't," she said, a firm wag of her head. "Not that I didn't want to." She looked at Roma. "I did very much. But my sons and their future came first. I worked hard, and thanks to those who gave me good advice, God bless them, I was able to put my sons through college and pay off the mortgage on the house."

Roma was reminded of her mother, a widow herself, who never missed an opportunity to relate her cares to anyone, be they willing or unwilling to listen. Unfortunately, that was where the resemblance ended.

Her companion had grown somber again. "Now both the boys are grown up and living their own lives. They have important jobs, therefore no time to give their mother a break so she can visit her family."

This was when the conversation would invariably come

to a halt. Mrs. Shah would turn to Roma with a look that she could only construe as a melancholic anticipation. It made her very uncomfortable.

What did Mrs. Shah want from her? Did she expect her to offer to take care of the shop? She wished she could help, but she felt incapable. Besides, her own life was so complicated. Roma would fidget in her seat and look at the door, hoping a customer would walk in.

Fortunately, Mrs Shah would start talking again. About random things— "Isn't the weather too hot?" or "Isn't the drizzle irritating?" How she missed chai and pakoras in the monsoon. The new Gujju restaurant downtown isn't too bad, you should check it out sometime, if you haven't yet. And the moment would pass.

"Oh, there you are. The vegetables are all set up," Mrs. Shah said.

Roma had stepped into a small alcove where various knick knacks such as cosmetics, soaps, henna, and bindis were on display.

"Okra looks very good this time," Mrs. Shah said. "I ordered the dark green ones, just like you said. I think I'll take some home with me today, rather than wait 'til tomorrow. My ancient neighbor, she's eighty by the way, has been requesting *bharva bhindi* for a while now."

Roma admired the okra. Long, slender green pods neatly arranged in parallel rows in the opened crate. They were fresh, therefore presumably good, yet she went through the process of selecting them individually. She bent their tips, applying slight pressure with her fingers and chose the ones that broke with a sharp snap.

"Is this any good?"

Roma looked up, startled.

A white woman, almost as tall as she was (and Roma was tall) stood in front of her with a box of frozen *palak paneer* in her hands. She was smartly turned out in a navy business suit and her red-gold hair was held up in a jaunty ponytail. An ID badge hung around her neck and said *Christine* in big bold letters. Everything was big, shining, and bold about her.

"Do you understand English?" Christine asked.

"Huh?" Roma realized she was staring. Embarrassed, she spoke fast. "Yes I do. Sorry, I can't help you. I don't cook frozen. Maybe Mrs. Shah, the owner would know better?"

The woman laughed. It was a full-throated hearty laugh. "According to her, this is better than what she cooks at home. Imagine that! Better than home? Unless she happens to be a really bad cook. Gosh, I love Indian food. I just wish I could make it somehow. It seems so complicated."

"Actually, it's quite easy. All you need is some basic ingredients. I can show you, if you wish," Roma said, wishing she hadn't when her offer was taken up.

"Is that a sari?" Christine asked.

Roma nodded.

"Do you mind if I touch it?"

Roma shook her head. She watched as the woman caressed the fabric, as if it was a rare artifact.

"It's beautiful, and you wear it so well."

Six yards of dyed cotton (synthetics irritated her skin, caused a rash, and made her sweat like a pig) that Roma chose to wrap around her gangly figure every day. She painstakingly washed it by hand, starched, (bought from Mrs. Shah's store) and dried by hanging on the railing over the bathtub (the apartment lacked a balcony). Why did she do it?

She couldn't come up with a simple explanation, but lately, she always wore a sari. Not the more convenient and universal salwar kurta but a sari. It was very unlike her. Back home until a few years ago, she had liked to dress like a tomboy and reap the disparaging remarks and wrath of her family. They should see her now. The sari

Under the Shade of the Banyan Tree

had become her symbol, her motif, the pristinely gathered pleats and perfectly arranged pallu.

Perhaps she wore it to help remind her of home, of the rebel she'd been, quietly putting her foot down. Or was it perhaps to infuriate Anand, who unfortunately did not react the way she'd expected him to, except maybe raise his eyebrows. On a couple of occasions, he'd grunted his disapproval when she tripped and almost took a terrible fall down the stairs hadn't he come to her aid in the nick of time. She sustained stares of various kinds, even from the fellow *desis* she met (many of whom considered the sari as an occasional garment). They were flabbergasted to know she hailed not from a small rural town, but from a large city. Even more, that she spoke fluent English. Their confusion made her smile.

* * *

The following week Roma postponed her excursion by a couple of hours to give Mrs. Shah enough time to arrange her wares and not throw her into a frenzy. It'd take a lot to throw the little woman into a frenzy, but Roma didn't want to take the risk.

She had made her calculations correctly when she saw a few customers leaving the store with bags full of produce. But she was in for a surprise. Christine (they had formally introduced themselves) was standing near the door and apparently waiting for her impatiently.

"The lady told me I'd find you here for sure, if I came by noon. It's almost one," Christine said in an accusatory tone.

"I'm sorry. Something came up. I was delayed," Roma said, sensing a familiar feeling of unease she hadn't experienced in years. It was as if Christine was the victim of an unknown crime that Roma had committed.

"You know that recipe you gave me for *Aloo Gobee?* I think I messed it up. I think I added a tablespoon of turmeric instead of a teaspoon, and a teaspoon of chili instead of a quarter. It was so awful I had to throw it all out. I tried it again with everything exact and perfect, but it didn't taste right. Not like it should. I'm no good."

Roma heaved a silent sigh of relief. The matter wasn't as dreadful as she thought. "I'm sure you missed something. Let's go over everything again step by step."

Christine shook her head. She had dressed down today. She was wearing grey shorts and a pink T with a large *Om* inscribed on it. Her beautiful hair lay in loose waves around her shoulders. She looked a lot less intimidating than the first day they had met.

"No, I can't do it," Christine said. "I'm sure I followed all the directions. I even cross-checked the recipe online. I think it needs the hands of an expert. It *needs* you. Can you come over to my place and show me how to do it?"

It was the most direct and honest request Roma had ever received. One she couldn't refuse. It was just one visit anyway.

* * *

Christine was a journalist. She was thirty-six and single. She lived in an apartment not far from the grocery store. It wasn't large—a small one bedroom, a cramped living room and kitchen. But it had a beautiful view of the lake.

"People say location is everything. I say, it's the view," Christine said.

What made the apartment look even smaller was a vast array of artifacts. There were African tribal masks, dolls, rugs, wooden bowls, various articles of jewelry, even a giant Indian headdress. "Spoils from my travels," Christine said mysteriously and didn't elaborate further.

The kitchen was tiny, like a shoebox, but neat. Roma nodded in approval when Christine showed her the new spice rack, precisely arranged and labeled. She also showed her a brand-new set of stainless steel pots and pans. She had even invested in a pressure cooker. "So you know I'm serious."

As Roma assembled the ingredients for the basic *desi* curry, Christine continued to talk.

"I used to work for a newspaper. It was back-breaking hard work, writing, researching, collecting news on all kinds of mundane boring things. I hated it and wanted to quit every day, but I had bills to pay. Then, I had a lucky break. I was witness to a bank robbery, you know the guys with the stockings covering their heads?"

Christine gestured with her hands and Roma nodded. "These men had something similar on, but it was thicker like a beanie and fit perfectly like a glove—like it was custom made. Custom made burglar masks, I'll be damned!"

Christine burst into her characteristic laugh. "You probably think it was no big deal. I should be thankful that I escaped unharmed, but guess what. One of these guys removed his beanie mask. He was having some kind of breathing problem like an asthma attack or something and I got a good look at his face before he ran. I remembered him." Christine had a huge grin on her face. "I happen to have a photographic memory. He was the same guy I'd interviewed for a story a while ago; he was a security guard at a local night club. That was enough for the cops to crack the case. They caught him, along with the rest of the gang and suddenly I'm famous!"

Christine disappeared into the bedroom and came back with a framed picture. "I was awarded the investigative journalist of the year award by the mayor, even though there wasn't much investigation involved."

She shrugged. "But hey, I took it and the small cash price that went with it. After that, I had many offers from a lot of different places—newspapers, magazines, even a local TV station. But I refused. I didn't want to work under anyone any more, so I went freelance. I get by."

Roma was dumbfounded. She understood now where Christine's confidence came from—the attractive radiance that had impressed her the very first time she'd met her. It came from her sense of self, her self-assurance. Roma felt insignificant in comparison. She looked down and started to chop the onions in a hurry.

"Do you live alone?" she said.

"Yes. I've had a few affairs. They didn't last long, except for one. Then I married him!" Christine burst out laughing again. "I couldn't breathe. He sucked all the oxygen from the room. I figured it's best to remain single."

"Are your parents okay with that?" Roma asked, glancing up at her.

"Why wouldn't they be? Anyway, I'm an adult. I'm my own woman. They can give me advise, but it's up to me to take it."

Roma didn't think she'd ever gain the temerity to take a similar stand with her mother. Indeed, she'd allowed herself to be molded by her like a piece of putty, so much so that she had barely any identity left.

"Enough about me," Christine said. "Tell me about you and your life. I bet it's a million times more interesting than mine."

"It isn't. You'll be bored." Roma turned the stove on.

"So, you won't tell me. You don't have to. Let me guess. I've been doing some research."

Roma watched curiously as Christine examined her face carefully and rubbed her black-beaded necklace between her fingers.

Under the Shade of the Banyan Tree

"Hmm. You are young, mid-twenties, have not been here long, a year at most? You've been married for almost the same time to a most wonderful young man, whom you hadn't met until just before your engagement. Who, by the way is, or shall I say was as innocent and inexperienced as you were before you got hitched. Am I right?" Christine winked at her.

Roma looked down at her hands.

Christine let out a joyful whoop. "Gosh, I find that so romantic! What's your husband's name? Or aren't you allowed to take it?"

Roma realized Christine's research was very behind the times.

"Anand...Anand Vaidyanathan."

Anand V like she used to call him. Roma had known her husband since she had been a little girl and unaware of the ways of the world. His family had moved into the big house next door when she was still in elementary school. The Vaidyanathans became the talk of the neighborhood. Mr. V wielded considerable influence as a high official in the government. His plump and pompous wife was a walking showroom of jewelry and Kancheepuram silks, while his only son rode to an exclusive private school every day in a chauffeured vehicle, but remained cloistered out of public view the rest of the time.

Infrequently though, Roma would catch glimpses of his pale bespectacled face while playing with her friends in her yard. This one day prompted her to waylay his mother and inquire if something dreadful ailed her son.

"Or else why doesn't he come out and play?" she asked innocently.

Mrs. V, considerably flustered at this impertinence, chose to walk away in a huff and her son vanished completely.

Hence, it was to Roma's utter surprise when Anand manifested in front of her with a soccer ball in his hands.

He followed it up the next day with a shining new cricket bat and ball. Apparently, it had taken him considerable courage to disrupt the barrier his mother had set up. His lack of speech made Roma believe he was mute, then she discovered he was painfully shy. A friendship blossomed between them. They were rarely seen apart. Roma taught her new friend how to climb trees and that it was okay to steal mangoes from Mr. Iyer's orchard (when he had so many, how could he miss a few). They swung from the roots of the old banyan tree in the temple yard, too.

Every evening, her mother would invite him into her kitchen and feed him mouth-watering North Indian delicacies. In turn, Anand helped Roma make sense of math and convert her Fs into Bs and As. This went on for a few years, despite Mrs. V's obvious disapproval.

Then he disappeared again. He had been packed off to a boarding school in Dehradun. Roma didn't hear from him until several years later when her mother informed her about his arrival. His proposal followed the next day. So, it wasn't exactly as Christine had said, but Roma wasn't about to correct her.

The curry turned out good. Christine was ecstatic. But she wasn't satisfied.

She grasped Roma's hands in hers. "I want to learn more. I want to become a gourmet cook so men will flock around me. Will you be willing to be my guru?"

Roma smiled and nodded. After all, at home she only had blank walls for company.

* * *

A few weeks later, Roma arrived at the usual time and found Christine already busy in the kitchen in a state of nervous excitement. She said she was throwing a lunch party.

Under the Shade of the Banyan Tree

"To test my newfound skills." She had invited a couple of her neighbors. "They are PhD students and always on the lookout for something free. Jill and Adam look like twins, but are actually husband and wife. I was shocked when they told me. You know there's a saying that if you live with someone long enough, you start looking like that person."

Roma wished her friend the best and took her leave, but Christine stopped her. "I insist. You haven't taught me how to make dessert."

* * *

"Is that all you do? Cook?" Stefano asked.

Roma felt as if something had stung her. Not just for the disparaging remark, but because it was the first thing Stefano had spoken to her. He had a distinct voice that grated on the ear like sandpaper.

When he stepped inside Christine's apartment, Roma had believed he was some kind of tramp who'd walked in from the street, pulled in by the irresistible aroma. She'd expected her friend to shoo him away. She was quite taken aback when she didn't. Instead, Stefano was welcomed with open arms like a long, lost friend and provided the seat of honor at the head of the table.

"Stefano is an artist," Christine said. "A realist, you know like Gustave Courbet?" she said with a gleeful wink.

When Roma didn't take the hint, Christine explained. "Stefano likes to get deep into his subject, which currently happens to be homelessness. He's living the life, as you can see."

What Roma saw was a man who looked like he hadn't had a square meal in days, nor had he bathed or groomed himself in a month—maybe more. It was all she could do to keep from covering her nose and mouth with her pallu. Stefano was obviously very sincere to his cause.

"What do you mean, Stef?" Christine asked. "Not everyone can cook."

"I didn't mean it that way, Chris. I think your new friend has other talents that she doesn't want to share. You don't have to take my word for it. Just look at her."

Roma squirmed on the edge of the sofa.

"You know, I think Stef is right," Adam said. "What are you hiding, Roma?"

"She has a lovely voice. Yes, I bet she sings!" Jill, his fragile bird-like wife twittered.

"Nah!" Stefano waved a hand dismissively. "This woman dances."

"Really?" Jill asked. "You dance Bollywood? Gosh, I love Bollywood. I've been a big fan ever since I saw Slumdog."

"Not that crap. Her art is deep. More refined," Stefano said, his eyes fixed on Roma.

Christine had been quiet so far. "Stefano's very intuitive," she said. "He's never wrong in such matters. Roma, you have to dance for us."

"I'm not good at all. Besides, I haven't danced in a long time." Roma looked imploringly at Christine.

"You have to," Christine said. "No excuses. Please, for your friend?"

Roma knew she was stuck. She closed her eyes to compose herself. Then, she slowly got up and tried to move her hands and feet in ways other than required for the most mundane tasks of daily life. It seemed like an eon had passed since she had taken up this activity, which she'd decided to give up forever. It turned out to be an embarrassing struggle and the movements ungainly and hideous. She could hear her guru's shrill admonishing tirade, even though the steps were among the most basic.

Under the Shade of the Banyan Tree

She couldn't go on and stopped almost on the edge of tears. When her small audience erupted in applause, she was certain they were mocking her.

* * *

"Roma? That's your name, isn't it?"

Roma paused at the door. She had been about to enter Shah Groceries. She stopped and scanned her surroundings. The voice was unmistakable, but she couldn't spot the owner.

"It's me, Stefano. We met at Chris' place. She told me where to find you."

The man talking to her was resting his long limbs against a lamp post across from the store. Roma regarded him with suspicion, then blushed with embarrassment. It wasn't her fault that she didn't recognize him.

The man had undergone a drastic transformation. Most of the facial hair was gone. What remained had been neatly combed away from the face and a short crisp beard covered his chin. The torn, stained rags had been replaced with a bright yellow T-shirt and jeans, and most importantly, there was no odor. The homeless phase was over, she guessed. She was unsure of what to make of the change. Tramps and hobos evoked pity and a certain fear in her that she was ashamed to admit, even revulsion. Now that he had abandoned that identity she had to begin all over again, which distressed her quite a bit.

"I'm glad I found you," he said, uncoiling himself. "I want to show you something. Come with me." He turned around and started down the crosswalk. He didn't give her a chance to refuse.

I could've ignored him. But she followed him.

"I live close by," he said, raising his voice above the

sounds of the street.

They walked a couple of blocks.

I could turn back now. But Roma kept on walking, intrigued. She trailed him through a filthy alley, then down a winding street, then across a bridge and another street. By the time he strode into a laundromat, Roma was thoroughly confused. She stood in the middle of the floor and glanced around, almost expecting someone to come forward and tell her what was going on and why she was here.

"Come on. Don't worry, I won't rape you." Stefano stood next to an open door at the back of the store that led to a flight of stairs.

Roma was glad he'd headed up and didn't see her blush.

At the top of the stairs, she followed him into a long narrow passage painted in vivid hues. The kaleidoscope of color threw Roma's head into a wild spin that she almost lost her balance. She closed her eyes, took a deep breath, then slowly opened them again. She was surrounded by pictures—thousands of them—posters, paintings, and murals. She turned around slowly. Most of them seemed to be related to music. She was arrested by one in particular. It had a black man depicted as Lord Vishnu in his most magnificent avatar.

"That's Jimi Hendrix. Cool, isn't it?" Stefano said softly behind her, making her jump. "But that's not what I want to show you. Come."

He pushed at a section of the wall at the end of the passage. It turned out to be a door and he waved her ahead.

Roma walked in after quite a bit of hesitation, preparing herself for another jolt. And surprised she was, as it was in stark contrast from the room she'd left behind. It was like she had been floundering in the sea and suddenly had been pulled onto dry land.

The room wasn't huge, but certainly more airy and filled with natural light. She saw images again, some on

Under the Shade of the Banyan Tree

easels, many tacked to the wall. There were drawings and sketches in black and white of people on the streets. Destitute souls scavenging among trash, sleeping on park benches, finding shelter under bridges, shooting up poison. They had a uniform look on their faces. Resignation. Their spirits had given in. It was all so real that Roma was moved. She noticed that many of the drawings were incomplete, like unvarnished wood, as if the artist had taken up the project, then given up prematurely. Was it by design or would he complete them at a later date?

"What do you think? Good enough for an exhibit?" he asked.

"Why do you ask? These are wonderful." She looked at him.

Stefano shook his head. "I don't think anyone will buy them. Too grim and ugly. They tell a story people don't want to see."

"I would, if I had the money." Roma smiled at him.

"Well, I'm flattered. And for saying so, you deserve a gift." He walked to the wall and removed a sketch of an old woman sitting on a roadside bench next to a shopping cart overflowing with all kinds of stuff.

"Sonya sat at the corner of this very street for so long that the day she disappeared I felt like a landmark had gone missing." He rolled up the picture and presented it to Roma. "Here, you can have her now."

"This is too generous. I can't."

"You have to. I need to empty this space for my next project." He winked at her.

"What happened to Sonya?" Roma asked, fingering the rolled sheet.

"She died. Or relocated to another spot. I don't know. Anyway, that is not why I brought you here." He hauled an easel from the back of the room, then set it in front of her. With a flourish, he flung back the cover. "This is."

Roma stared. "Is that me?"

"Yes."

She stepped forward and without seeking permission, gently touched the sinuous silhouette of the dancer. There was an extraordinary joy in her movement that felt alien to Roma. But the rendering was incomplete. The space where the dancer's likeness should have been had been left blank. She had a good idea why.

"What happened? Do you think it's not good enough?"

She glanced at him. "No. It is very good."

Stefano smiled. "I see you noticed. My dancer lacks a face. I wanted to put you there, but I didn't want to do it from memory. I want you to sit for me. I can't leave this lovely woman incomplete."

Roma shook her head. "You can put anyone there. Doesn't have to be me." She turned and started for the door.

"It *has* to be you. No one else." Stefano blocked her way. "Besides, I find your face very interesting and unique. It'll make the painting special. I can compensate you for your time, if you wish."

"I don't want your money. I'll do it, so you can finish the job," Roma said. "That's all."

"That's the spirit. Let's begin ASAP. How about tomorrow at one?"

Roma didn't tell Stefano the reason why she'd agreed to sit for him was because he'd said he found her interesting and unique. It sounded better than plain and dowdy. That, and because she found Stefano to be an enigma himself. Carefree and flamboyant on the outside, but earnest and deep on the inside—like his apartment. There was a lot more to this man.

Roma hid the present on the top of the kitchen closet where she knew it was unlikely for Anand to find it. She opened her suitcase and removed her dancing bells from the very bottom where she had hidden them. She hadn't touched them since she had arrived in the States nearly five months ago.

She bent down and tied them around her ankles. The weight felt strange. She walked around the apartment, rejoicing in their lilting chime. She began to hum. What should I cook for dinner? She opened the refrigerator. And for the meeting with Stefano tomorrow? What'd he like?

* * *

Before she saw it, she smelled it. It was more overpowering than the stuffed parathas she'd made. It was the distinct fragrance of incense. A lot of it. Stefano had stuck a huge poster of Kali on his wall.

"I love Hindu Gods," he said as Roma surveyed the makeshift altar that held the deities of Ganesh and Shiva. "How many do you have? A million? They are so laissez faire. They leave you to your karma. No interference. Perfect for me."

Roma had never thought of her religion that way. She had silently followed the rituals and said her prayers. Perhaps Stefano was right. She wished her parents had taught her more.

Stefano had placed a barstool in front of the easel, but he didn't restrict her to it. He told her to wander around as she pleased, though sometimes, he asked her to hold a certain stance or look a certain way. He surprised her one day by playing an old Indian tune—something Roma hadn't heard in a very long time and she was instantly captivated. Her eyes closed and unknowingly, she began to sway to the music.

It was D day.

The day when Stefano had said he'd finish the painting. He was taking his own sweet time about it. He removed a thin reed out of a box, lit it, and puffed on it 'til the end glowed red. She recognized it as a beedi.

"Good unadulterated poison. Want some?" he asked.

She shook her head and tried not to breathe in the fumes.

He laughed and puffed vigorously, gazing at the ceiling. His eyes glazed over in the dense smoke. His face looked disembodied. Inhuman.

Roma shivered.

"Don't you folks smoke this, or are you pretending to be a prude?"

Roma stood up. "If not smoking is being a prude, then I'm not pretending."

He waved her back down and stubbed the reed out. "I was just sorting you out. Cataloging you. I think I've figured you out."

"You have?" She sat forward.

"A frigid virgin. Even though you're married."

Her mouth dropped open.

"And you'll remain one till you find..." He didn't complete the sentence. "Then all that passion will erupt like Vesuvius. Bad news. But I like bad news."

Roma got up and stalked toward the door. "You've insulted me. I'm leaving."

"Before you see your painting? I don't think so." He turned the easel around.

Roma stared at the woman in the portrait and her chest started to pound. It was as if she was looking in the mirror, but the image was different. It wasn't her.

Suddenly, Stefano grabbed both her arms and pinned her to the wall. He began to kiss her.

The abrupt assault incapacitated Roma. Her body felt lifeless, as if she was free-falling into an endless abyss. It took considerable fortitude to wrench her face away. "Why are you doing this?"

"Because I'm infatuated with you. As are you with me. Don't deny it."

Under the Shade of the Banyan Tree

"No." She tried to push him away, but he was too strong.

"Of course you are. Don't act naïve. Or else why would you come to a stranger's house, a man you barely know. Why would you bring me all that delicious food. Because your husband doesn't give you what you want. Right?"

"No!" Roma screamed. She kicked wildly with her legs and managed to connect, then took the opportunity to free herself and escape.

She ran helter skelter through the streets, blinded by her tears. She was ashamed and disappointed with herself. She'd been living in a fairytale. Had she expected someone to come by and sweep her off my feet? Had she led Stefano on? Then why hadn't she welcomed his advances? Why did his touch make her flesh crawl? But what he'd said about her had hit close to home.

* * *

Roma and Anand had got married on a cold day in December. It was a neat little ceremony; a sweet amalgam of both north and south Indian traditions that had sent the attendees into throes of ecstasy. Their nuptial night had been spent in the company of friends and family. Her new spouse promptly left after accompanying her to the US Embassy the following day, ensuring she filed her visa application.

Roma had settled down for a long wait. Therefore, she was surprised when a few months later the all clear was given and frantic preparations were made for her to join her husband. No one had more delight than her mother, Sukanya devi.

Anand lived in a small but comfortable one-bedroom

apartment in Evanston, a city north of Chicago. He had gone to school there and was now employed as an associate professor in the department of chemical engineering.

Their living situation had initially thrown her into confusion. Then she had chided herself. Anand was no longer her friend. He was her husband and she his wife. Roma had closed her eyes to receive his first kiss. It had surprised her when he kissed her with unexpected force and roughness. He'd withdrawn when he sensed her stiffen, then got up and left.

There were a few more attempts. Well, not really.

Anand had realized that the definitions of their relationship had changed. She was no longer his best friend with whom he could talk to or even touch innocently.

He confronted her one day, a couple of weeks after her arrival. Enough time for jet lag to have dissipated and for both of them to have reconciled to the newness of their relationship.

"Okay, tell me. Why did you agree to marry me?" he asked sincerely.

Roma was taken aback. She hadn't expected the question, especially after a breakfast of soft fluffy idlis she'd made for him with dough she had prepared after much toil the day before using an American food processor.

"I thought you were fond of me," he went on. "We were good friends, or was I mistaken?"

Not just good friends. *Very good friends.* "Yes, we were good friends," she said, "but that isn't the same as being husband and wife or…lovers."

He had the grace to look uncomfortable.

She said she'd accepted his proposal at the behest of her mother. "It has been her rant ever since father passed away. You know she's a simple woman. She had started to worry I'd die a spinster. A spinster at twenty-six!" Roma laughed.

Under the Shade of the Banyan Tree

She didn't tell him that when her father departed (his liver finally succumbing to his alcohol habit) a few years after Mrs. V had dispatched Anand off to boarding school, she felt she'd lost her only remaining friend. The trauma went deeper when Sukanya devi had to mortgage their home and sell most of her jewelry to clear his innumerable debts. Roma was forced to quit college in favor of her beautiful and smart (hence, more deserving) younger sibling and pick up odd jobs to support the family. Her mother also made her give up her dance lessons, even when her guru agreed to teach her for free. He'd seen a brilliant future for her.

"He's lying. You could be a Kali, but never a Shakuntala. Anyway, society would never approve," her mother said.

Roma also didn't tell Anand why Sukanya Devi was worried sick her eldest daughter would never get married. Her dusky skin and unusual height made her an undesirable match and her mother loved to rub it in. She didn't care that each time she did so she ran an ice-cold knife into Roma's heart. She'd even mentioned she wouldn't be unhappy if Roma followed in her sister Rashmi's footsteps who'd run away and eloped with her forty-some year-old boss.

"At least he's rich. But with your looks, you'll be lucky to entrap a ruffian off the street."

Therefore, when Anand's proposal came, it was as if the almighty himself had intervened.

That was that. Anand's half-baked attempts at advancing their relationship ended. He slept on the living room couch. Their conversations were brief, except when absolutely necessary or when he couldn't help but admire her cooking.

"You don't have to go to extra lengths to cook for me," he'd remind her more than a few times a week.

Each time, Roma responded by saying she liked to cook. It kept her occupied.

* * *

Roma woke with a start. "Are you okay?"

Anand had cracked the bedroom door open.

"Yes, I'm fine. I think I fell asleep. I'll be right out." Anand withdrew, closing the door behind him. The room was pitch dark.

She realized she'd rushed back home after the afternoon's misadventure and crashed on the bed and cried herself to sleep. Roma looked at her face in the bathroom mirror and splashed it several times with cold water. But the wretched feeling wouldn't go away. What did she expect? Anand wasn't to blame. He had never forced himself on her. It was she who had been living in some kind of fantasy. She screamed internally at herself. *Get real Roma! Get real!*

When she walked out, dinner was already laid out. She felt Anand watching her as they ate.

"Is something wrong?" he asked.

Yes, everything is wrong. You, me, us. She shook her head.

"If you want to go back home, you can. I won't hold you back. You're not my prisoner."

"No, I'm fine here. Just fine." Roma was overcome with guilt. He had been thinking about her.

He sat back and sighed. "I think I'll turn in. Have an early class tomorrow."

Later, back in the bedroom, she couldn't sleep. She couldn't understand why her spouse felt obligated to care for her. Was it all due to a simple ceremony? The world was such a terrible place. It bound people in artificial relationships that were so difficult to be rid of.

Her thoughts competed with the tick tock of the clock.

It was one AM and she could see the living room light was still on. He hadn't been able to sleep, either.

Anand was lying on the carpet on his makeshift bed next to the sofa, the NYT open on his chest.

She hadn't realized he slept on the floor since he was always up before she was. He had fallen asleep without taking off his glasses.

Roma removed them gingerly, then reached down to smooth back the shock of hair from his forehead but held herself back.

* * *

The following evening, she hung around in the living room at the usual time, impatient for his arrival home. He was late, and her nervousness compounded with every minute that passed. Had she angered him by testing his patience beyond that of any regular human being could tolerate?

Of course, she had. And she had toyed with his feelings. That, too, without offering any excuses for her behavior.

When he returned a good two hours later, her eyes anxiously probed his face while reheating the food she had prepared with great care. It was a serious face and not unpleasant at all. The hollow bony planes of boyhood had filled in to form a lean, elegant profile and his pale skin had gained a healthy tan. Her gawky, bashful childhood friend had grown into a good-looking responsible man. So, what was he doing with her?

Anand looked oblivious to her scrutiny or he was doing a good job of making it appear so. He praised the food like he hadn't done so before. It meant something was amiss and that upset her.

"By the way, I'll be back early tomorrow. A friend of mine has invited us for dinner."

"Someone from back home?" Roma asked.

"No. Someone I knew in college." Anand didn't say more.

* * *

Roma chose a silk sari in cobalt blue and gold. It was a special occasion. Before today, she hadn't met any of Anand's friends or acquaintances. It was important to make a good impression. If they were Indians, they were sure to report back home. She added a simple gold necklace and *jhumkas* to complete the look.

The 'friend' lived almost two hours away, in a small town across the border in Wisconsin. Anand looked preoccupied and unwilling to share any further information. The scenery whizzed by—lush green forests and vast tracts of farmland. Roma wondered who she was *actually* trying to impress.

They stopped before a neat little house with a lovely yard full of shade trees and flowers in bloom. The door was opened by a young oriental man holding a crying baby in his arms. He introduced himself as Kevin, Rosalie's husband.

Roma was baffled. Anand's 'friend' was a woman.

Kevin invited them inside to sit in the spacious living room and hurried away, saying he needed to change the baby.

"Nice house, isn't it?" Anand said.

Roma didn't reply. She was busy twisting the end of her sari around her fingers.

Rosalie breezed in, all smiles. She first rushed to Anand and hugged him, then came up to Roma and shook her hand.

Under the Shade of the Banyan Tree

"At last! I've been wanting to meet you for so long," Rosalie said.

She was all Roma had expected and more—beautiful, pristinely clothed, articulate, and a devoted wife. She taught English at the local community college.

"I was never as smart as Anand to be hired by the Uni. Kevin had a secure job with the city, so I compromised."

Kevin returned, minus the baby. "Shall we eat? I'm starved."

Roma pushed the food around her plate. It was delicious, but she had no appetite.

The conversation flowed around the table warm and cozy, like the red wine Rosalie was serving.

Roma didn't contribute much, choosing to remain silent for the most part. Instead, she observed her husband. He was a revelation—laughing, talking in sentences longer than a few words, even making jokes. He reminded her of her old friend who she believed had disappeared a long time ago.

After dinner, Kevin dragged Anand to the basement to show off his one-of-a-kind game room. Rosalie was going to check on the baby.

"You're welcome to join me, unless you prefer to hang out with the boys." She smiled at Roma.

They sat side by side on the futon in the nursery while the baby slept in her crib.

Rosalie was a native of California, born and raised, one of eight children. Her parents were immigrants from China. "We're very close. My parents and siblings all live within miles of each other. I really miss them." She sighed, then abruptly looked at Roma. "What am I saying. You must be really homesick. I am, even though I'm just a few hours away."

Roma nodded, wondering if her host would be shocked if she said she hardly missed home at all.

Rosalie went on without missing a beat. She talked

about how tough it used to be for immigrants and how things were changing. She talked about her upbringing; how stern and old-fashioned her parents were.

"So, I believe all Asian parents are, don't you agree?"

She talked about college.

Roma pricked her ears.

"Anand is so smart. He's probably the smartest guy I've met. And such a charmer. He'd hardly open his mouth in college but when he did, he'd knock us all for a loop." She blushed. "You know, I was so taken by him that I went ahead and proposed to him one day."

She laughed. "That man broke my heart. He was so rude. He promptly refused, saying there was someone back home." She smiled at Roma. "Now I see why he said so."

It was late when they started back home. The blazing marmalade sky was turning quickly to dusk. Anand heeded Kevin's advice and took the county road to bypass the crowded highway. After a few miles, the city lights disappeared and they were surrounded by a vast unbroken emptiness.

Anand turned on the radio and began to scan through the channels before finally settling on smooth jazz.

Roma reached forward to turn up the volume so the music could help displace the noise in her head.

She must have drifted off, for when she opened her eyes, the car had come to a standstill. She couldn't see anything because they were enclosed by a thick wall of gray.

Suddenly, there was a huge roar and she let out a shriek as big chunks of ice began pelting the front windshield.

Anand reached over and drew her tight to his chest. "It's all right, Roma. Just a hailstorm."

Roma relaxed in his warmth and slowly breathed in his scent. It was raw, earthy, and utterly magnetic.

The storm passed, but the impact of Anand's embrace

stayed with Roma. They made it to the apartment in record time.

"I'm going for a walk. Don't wait up for me." Anand stalked out, banging the door shut behind him.

She wanted to run after him and say she was sorry. Instead, she leaned against the window that looked onto the street.

She'd been wrong. It wasn't pity that had prompted Anand to take her as his wife. He hadn't forced himself into a relationship just to fulfill an imagined duty to rescue a friend (who also happened to be the ugly daughter of a widow of poor means) from a life of loneliness and hardship.

She caught her reflection in the glass. Stefano's portrait was coming to life.

Anand returned sometime after midnight. She could hear him tossing and turning until the wee hours of the morning. Then he began to pace up and down the hallway and nearly knocked her over when she stepped out of the bedroom after her shower. He looked haggard and she was overcome with remorse. She wanted to hug him, but restrained herself.

"What do you want for breakfast?" she asked, trying hard to sound matter-of-fact.

"Hmm?"

"I said breakfast."

"Oh. Anything."

"Okay then, I'll make dosa." She tucked her sari around her waist and opened the refrigerator. "I made the mango chutney yesterday. The kind that you like so much. Mrs. Shah had some really nice raw mangoes in the store."

"Roma, we need to talk."

"What did you say?"

"We need to talk. It's something important."

She turned around. He had his hands planted on the counter and his face looked grim.

"Can't we talk later?" she asked. "After breakfast."

"No, we need to talk now. Come sit down." He took her arm and gently led her to the couch.

She began to tremble. What did he want to talk about? Divorce? Sending her back to India? No, that can't be. She looked around for some kind of distraction. A colorful pamphlet on the coffee table caught her eye. It had come along with yesterday's mail. Anand had yet to sort it. She snatched it up.

"Roma...we..."

"Anand. Look, there's a carnival in town. Have you been to one here? Are they like what we have back home?" she asked, meeting his eyes.

"I don't know."

"It sounds like so much fun. I really want to go. Will you take me? Today?"

He looked perplexed.

"It isn't far. We could walk."

* * *

No one can ever be unhappy at a carnival. The sights and sounds, hustle and bustle, children running around, their laughter and carefree shrieks, are enough to brighten any mood and tease a smile from even the most devout pessimist.

Roma's companion was a different species altogether. Nothing so far had piqued his interest. He didn't even blink when the knife juggler they'd been watching for the past half hour misjudged a throw and nearly sliced his arm in half. She was sure he was thinking about their interrupted conversation from that morning. It was only a matter of time before he brought it up again and she wouldn't be able to avert it.

A loud cheer erupted, signaling an end to the act.

Anand tipped the man and they started to walk again. Roma spotted some people eating cotton candy and wondered aloud if she should try some.

"Sure," he said. "Why don't you."

It took her a while to decide on a flavor. There were so many choices. The look on her face as the candy melted in her mouth forced a smile out of Anand.

"It's not like what we have back home," she said. "Try some."

"It isn't?"

She took another bite of the sugar cloud. "No. Don't you remember Venkat mama? He used to come by with his cart every winter. Rashmi and I'd beg Dad to buy us some every weekend. That stopped after he passed away, but the memory of the flavor still remains with me."

Anand shrugged. "Mom never let me have it. She said I'd get sick. Now, don't look at me like that. I was just a kid and Mom, you know very well how overbearing she can get."

Roma broke a large chunk of pink colored floss and offered it to him. "Try it. You're not a kid anymore. Nor is your mom here."

It wasn't clear if the spun sugar treat had gained a new fan, but Anand was a lot more upbeat afterwards. There was a new spring in his step, and he was smiling, actually *smiling*.

Now they were walking side by side, close enough that their arms brushed. Roma's heart started to beat faster.

Anand pointed to a stand where several people were in line, trying to guess the weight of a giant pumpkin. He looked at her. "Why don't you give it a shot?"

She did and was only off by a few pounds.

Anand tried his luck at the shooting gallery. He missed quite a few balloons but did well with the ring toss. He won a goldfish that he presented to Roma.

She turned and offered it to a little girl who had been watching him with her blue eyes big and round. She snapped it up with a loud squeal of joy.

They rode the giant Ferris wheel. Roma clung to his arm when they swayed on top waiting for the passengers to unload. He laughed when she asked if they could go again. This time he wrapped his arm around her waist and pointed out the landmarks in the glittering skyline.

The rides had closed for the day and the merchants were packing up.

"Looks like it's time to go home," Anand said. There was a quiet intensity in his eyes that made Roma shiver.

They hurried by some stragglers creating a ruckus in the unpaved parking lot with their headlights on. The wind blew through the empty streets, kicking up a cloud of dust.

Roma heard the sound of distant thunder. She drew her sari over her head and giggled as they ran to the bus stop. But the unsubstantial shelter offered little escape from the light shower that quickly turned into a steady drizzle. As the rain gathered strength, the street rapidly transformed into a shallow river.

"I'd better call a taxi," Anand said and reached for his phone. "What are you doing? You'll get sick!" he blurted out as Roma stepped out and stretched out her arms and turned her face to the sky.

"Not I. You will, mama's boy!" She laughed.

He grinned and joined her. "What say we race back home for old times' sake?"

She accepted his challenge, but it wasn't easy going even when she hitched her sari up above her knees. The water was coming down in sheets. Anand was often at her side to give her a hand, and sometimes to lug her across suspicious bodies of water.

An eerie silence greeted them back at the apartment. The clamor of the rain receding into the background splattering the walls like tiny missiles; drum rolls that revved up into a crescendo then grew muffled before finally settling into a steady rhythm—the rhythm of Roma's heart.

The carpet was ruined but Roma didn't want to think about it. She stood in the hallway waiting as Anand closed and locked the door. She felt him behind her, close, and it made her dizzy. The tension in her bosom eased slightly as the knot in one of the strings of her blouse came undone.

"Roma?" His voice was soft, hopeful.

With an exasperated gasp, she abruptly swung around and flung her arms around his neck. "We should get rid of these clothes before both of us catch the death of cold. Don't you agree?"

"Absolutely," he said, his smile banishing all her doubts and misgivings.

The off-center dot

The unruly locks

The provocative pout

The askew dress

The wayward hand

The caressing squeeze

The deliberate kiss

The capricious heart

A Cup of Tea

A cup of tea
is a fuzzy, warm morning
flicking aside the blanket of night
It is a lazy afternoon
a let's sit down
and chat for a while
It is a moment
booked just for me
to waste as I please
to brood
sit by the window
look at nothing
or hitchhike on a plume of steam
to neverland

If you enjoyed reading *Under the Shade of the Banyan Tree*, you may enjoy reading a poetry collection by award-winning author, Diamante Lavendar.

Poetry and Ponderings

Diamante Lavendar

A raw collection of poetry and prose based on one woman's experiences of being abused and how she healed herself to move past the assaults that happened to her. Diamante Lavendar, a victim of abuse, shows the reader the raw emotions of pain, hate, and denial that occur before a victim can heal. She shares these inspiring poems in hopes that it may help other victims heal their hurts, as she did while writing the collection.

Acknowledgements

I find poems to be very personal. So, it took quite a bit of courage to share them with my readers on my blog. I was pleasantly surprised with the response. Many told me the poems spoke to them and resonated with their feelings. They encouraged me to write more. In particular, I'm grateful to my dear friend, Anica, for bolstering my ego and helping me bring this collection to fruition.

—Simi K. Rao
Summer, 2019

ABOUT THE AUTHOR

Simi K. Rao was born and grew up in India before relocating to the U.S., where she has lived for several years. The inspiration for her books, and other projects, comes from her own experience with cross-cultural traditions, lifestyles and familial relationships. Rao enjoys exploring the dynamics of contemporary American culture blended with Indian customs and heritage to reflect the challenges and opportunities many Indian-American women face in real life. She is a practicing physician, and much of Rao's down time is devoted to creative pursuits, including writing fiction and poetry, and photography. She is also an avid traveler and has visited many locations around the world. She has written four novels, one of which is *The Accidental Wife,* and is currently working on a new novel. To learn more about her or her books, visit SimiKRao.com or find her on Facebook.

www.ingramcontent.com/pod-product-compliance
Lightning Source LLC
Chambersburg PA
CBHW030117100526
44591CB00009B/436